Beyond the Surface:
Exploring Love, Intimacy, Infatuation & Sex

Sex

 *Beyond the Surface: Exploring Love, Intimacy, Infatuation & Sex; The Sex Series* is from a psychological perspective that offers a profound and nuanced exploration of human sexuality, delving into the emotional, mental, and relational dimensions that shape intimate connections. Far beyond a superficial understanding of sex, this eBook provides readers with an in-depth examination of how psychological factors influence desire, intimacy, and the complexities of sexual relationships.

The book begins by unraveling the intricate web of attraction and connection, exploring how our past experiences, attachment styles, and cultural narratives shape the way we perceive and engage in sexual relationships. It emphasizes the dynamic interplay between physical and emotional intimacy, illustrating how both are vital for fulfilling connections. As it unfolds, the narrative invites readers to reflect on their own sexual identities, the power of self-perception, and the barriers that often hinder true intimacy.

With compassion and clarity, this eBook addresses challenges such as mismatched desires, communication breakdowns, and the impact of stress and mental health on sexual well-being. It offers readers the psychological tools to better understand themselves and their partners, encouraging open dialogue and a deeper appreciation of vulnerability in relationships. By combining insights from psychology with practical advice, it equips couples and individuals to grow, heal, and foster lasting connections rooted in trust and mutual respect.

This work is not merely a guide to improving sexual relationships but a thoughtful meditation on the deeper forces that drive our most intimate experiences. Whether you are seeking to reignite passion, understand your own desires, or strengthen the bond with a partner, this book serves as a compassionate and enlightening resource. It invites readers to look beyond the surface and embrace the profound, transformative potential of human sexuality.

Chapter 1: The Foundations of Sexual Connections

- **The Psychology of Attraction:**
  Understanding the mental processes behind initial attraction, including evolutionary and cultural factors that shape sexual preferences.
- **Emotional Intimacy vs. Physical Intimacy:**
  Differentiating emotional closeness and sexual intimacy, and how they interconnect in healthy relationships.
- **The Role of Attachment Styles:**
  How attachment theory influences our sexual behaviors and needs, from secure bonds to anxieties in intimacy.

Chapter 2: Sex and Self-Perception

- **Body Image and Sexual Confidence:**
  Exploring the impact of body positivity, self-esteem, and personal insecurities on sexual satisfaction.
- **Sexual Identity and Self-Expression:**
  Navigating personal identity, orientation, and how societal pressures shape sexual behaviors and desires.
- **The Role of Mental Health:**
  Examining the influence of anxiety, depression, and stress on sexual functioning and relationships.

Chapter 3: The Psychology of Desire

- **Differentiating Love, Lust, and Infatuation:**
  Psychological distinctions between emotional connection, physical desire, and fleeting obsession.
- **Factors That Enhance or Diminish Desire:**
  Examining external and internal factors such as stress, communication, novelty, and emotional intimacy.
- **The Science of Sexual Compatibility:**
  Analyzing how personality traits, preferences, and emotional alignment affect long-term sexual harmony.

Chapter 4: Challenges and Growth in Sexual Relationships

- **Overcoming Sexual Communication Barriers:**
  Techniques for discussing needs, boundaries, and desires openly and without judgment.
- **Healing Sexual Disconnects:**
  Addressing issues like mismatched libidos, sexual boredom, or past traumas to rebuild intimacy.

- **Navigating the Impact of Life Stages:**
  How aging, parenthood, and health changes affect sexual dynamics and ways to adapt together.

Chapter 5: Building a Holistic Sexual Connection

- **The Role of Trust and Vulnerability:**
  Fostering emotional safety as the foundation for a fulfilling sexual relationship.
- **Exploring Sexual Growth Together:**
  Introducing ways couples can grow sexually, including exploring fantasies, trying new experiences, and attending workshops.
- **Cultivating Long-Term Intimacy:**
  Strategies for maintaining sexual and emotional connections over time, balancing routine with excitement.

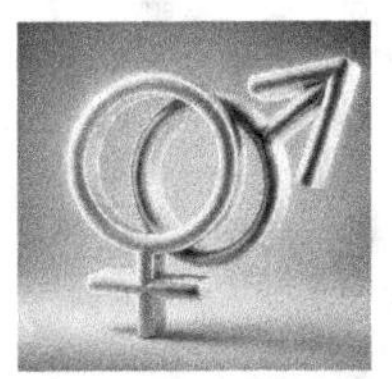

The Psychology of Attraction: Understanding the Mental Processes Behind Initial Attraction, Including Evolutionary and Cultural Factors That Shape Sexual Preferences

The psychology of attraction is a fascinating subject that delves into the intricate interplay of biological, psychological, and cultural factors that dictate how and why we are drawn to certain individuals. Attraction is influenced by evolutionary imperatives that have shaped human preferences over millennia, as well as by the cultural frameworks that provide meaning and context to these preferences. Understanding the mental processes behind initial attraction requires a nuanced exploration of these forces, as well as the ways they intersect in shaping our desires and decisions.

From an evolutionary standpoint, attraction is fundamentally tied to the survival and reproduction of the species. Certain traits, such as physical symmetry, have historically been associated with health and genetic fitness, making them universally appealing across cultures. For example, clear skin, bright eyes, and well-proportioned features often signal an absence of disease or genetic disorders, which would be advantageous for the survival of offspring. This evolutionary lens also explains preferences for characteristics that suggest fertility, such as youthful appearances in women or strength and resources in men. These biological predispositions are deeply ingrained, often operating beneath the level of conscious awareness. Yet, they do not exist in isolation; instead, they interact dynamically with the individual's personal experiences and the cultural milieu they inhabit.

Cultural factors also play a profound role in shaping and refining these innate preferences. While evolution provides a broad framework for what humans find attractive, culture dictates the specifics. In certain societies, ideals of beauty and desirability can vary dramatically. Western media has often celebrated slim, tall figures, other cultures have prized fuller body types as symbols of wealth and health. Similarly, the emphasis on certain physical attributes, such as facial hair in men or specific body shapes in women, is largely determined by cultural narratives and media representation. These ideals are not static but evolve over time, reflecting changes in societal values, economic conditions, and technological advances. Cultural norms and media images can either amplify or suppress biological tendencies, creating a complex feedback loop between nature and nurture in the domain of attraction.

On a psychological level, attraction is also shaped by individual experiences, memories, and subconscious associations. Early attachments formed during childhood can profoundly influence the types of people one finds attractive as an adult. For instance, those who experienced warmth and security in their primary relationships may gravitate toward partners who exude similar qualities. Conversely, unresolved conflicts or traumas can lead individuals to seek out partners who unconsciously recreate these dynamics, whether for resolution or repetition. Beyond personal history, the brain's reward system plays a pivotal role in attraction. When we encounter someone we find appealing, our brain releases a cocktail of neurotransmitters, including dopamine and oxytocin, which create feelings of pleasure and attachment. This biochemical process not only reinforces attraction but also encourages behaviors that deepen the bond, such as spending time together or engaging in shared activities.

Another significant factor in the psychology of attraction is the role of similarity and familiarity. Humans are often drawn to those who share their values, interests, or backgrounds, as these commonalities create a sense of safety and predictability. This phenomenon, known as the "similarity-attraction effect," is rooted in the idea that shared traits foster understanding and reduce potential conflicts. At the same time, familiarity also plays a crucial role in attraction. Studies have shown that repeated exposure to a person increases their appeal, a phenomenon known as the "mere exposure effect." It explains why people often develop romantic feelings for colleagues, classmates, or others they see regularly. However, while similarity and familiarity are powerful forces, they are often balanced by the allure of novelty and mystery, which can spark curiosity and excitement.

The psychology of attraction is also influenced by situational factors, such as proximity and timing. Physical closeness often facilitates connection by increasing the opportunities for interaction and emotional bonding, which is why many romantic relationships begin in shared environments, such as workplaces, schools, or neighborhoods. Timing is equally critical, as individuals are more likely to be receptive to attraction when they are emotionally available and seeking connection. Furthermore, contextual elements, such as stress or heightened emotions, can intensify attraction. An example of this would be when people who meet in high-adrenaline situations, like on a roller coaster or during a shared challenge, are more likely to report a stronger connection due to the physiological arousal associated with the experience.

In examining the psychology of attraction, it becomes clear that this seemingly simple phenomenon is, in reality, an intricate tapestry woven from biological imperatives, cultural influences, and psychological intricacies. The interplay between these elements not only shapes who we are drawn to but also reveals deeper truths about the human condition. Attraction is not merely a matter of personal preference; it is a window into the ways our past, present, and environment converge to guide our most intimate choices.

Emotional Intimacy vs. Physical Intimacy:
Differentiating Emotional Closeness and Sexual Intimacy, and How They Interconnect in Healthy Relationships

Emotional intimacy and physical intimacy are two integral dimensions of human relationships, each offering its unique way of fostering closeness, connection, and fulfillment. While they are often intertwined, they are distinct in nature, functioning on different planes of human experience. Emotional intimacy delves into the realm of feelings, thoughts, and vulnerability, creating a space where individuals feel safe and seen. In contrast, physical intimacy is rooted in the sensory and bodily connection between people, often encompassing expressions of touch, affection, and sexual interaction. Together, they can form the foundation of a deeply bonded relationship, but their interplay and independence deserve thoughtful exploration.

Emotional intimacy is the bedrock of trust and understanding in a relationship. It consists of a profound connection that transcends physical presence, allowing partners to share their innermost fears, dreams, and experiences without fear of judgment. This type of closeness is cultivated over time through open communication, empathy, and mutual respect. It's a dynamic process where individuals feel secure enough to let down their guard and reveal their true selves. Emotional intimacy is not solely about talking; it is also about listening and responding in ways that affirm and validate the other person's feelings. It's in the shared silences, the exchanged glances that say more than words ever could, and the unwavering support during moments of vulnerability.

This connection can exist independently of physical intimacy, underscoring its unique role in relationships. For example, close friends may experience deep emotional intimacy without any physical component. However, in romantic partnerships, the presence of emotional intimacy often enriches physical expressions of affection. When individuals feel emotionally secure, the barriers to physical closeness tend to dissolve, paving the way for a more profound and authentic experience of physical intimacy. This demonstrates the interplay between the two forms of closeness, where emotional bonding can act as a precursor to physical connection.

Physical intimacy, on the other hand, encompasses a spectrum of actions that convey love, attraction, and desire. Since sexual activity is a significant aspect of physical intimacy, it is by no means the entirety of it. Holding hands, hugging, cuddling, or even a light touch on the arm can all serve as powerful ways of building physical closeness. Unlike emotional intimacy, which often requires significant time to develop, physical intimacy can sometimes spark spontaneously, driven by chemistry and immediate attraction. Yet, in the absence of emotional intimacy, the connection derived from physical closeness may feel hollow or fleeting.

For relationships to thrive, physical intimacy often needs to be supported by emotional depth. When partners are emotionally distant or harbor unresolved conflicts, physical touch can feel disconnected, mechanical, or even uncomfortable. Conversely, when emotional intimacy is strong, physical expressions of love are imbued with meaning and authenticity. A kiss becomes more than a kiss; it becomes a tangible affirmation of love, trust, and belonging. This interplay highlights how emotional and physical intimacy, though distinct, often enhance and reinforce one another.

However, the interconnection between emotional and physical intimacy is not always straightforward. Some relationships may face challenges when one form of intimacy outpaces the other. Partners who are emotionally intimate but lack a satisfying physical connection might feel as though an essential element is missing from their relationship. Similarly, those who rely heavily on physical intimacy without fostering emotional closeness may struggle to sustain a deep and enduring bond. In such cases, the balance between these two dimensions becomes crucial. Recognizing their individual and collective importance can help partners navigate the complexities of their relationship and address unmet needs.

In healthy relationships, the integration of emotional and physical intimacy creates a cycle of mutual reinforcement. Emotional closeness encourages physical expressions of love, and in turn, these physical acts deepen emotional bonds. This dynamic interplay fosters a sense of wholeness in the relationship, allowing partners to feel both desired and deeply valued. It is this balance that transforms a connection from surface-level to profound, nurturing not only the relationship itself but also the individual well-being of those involved.

Understanding and appreciating the distinction and connection between emotional and physical intimacy is essential for anyone seeking a meaningful relationship. Each plays a vital role, and both require intention and effort to cultivate. The path to emotional intimacy may involve patience, vulnerability, and trust-building, the journey toward physical intimacy often necessitates openness, respect, and attunement to each other's boundaries and desires. Together, they form the pillars of enduring and fulfilling relationships, offering a sanctuary of connection in an increasingly disconnected world.

When emotional and physical intimacy are in harmony, they create a partnership that is not only deeply satisfying but also resilient against the trials of life. Such relationships become a testament to the beauty of human connection in its fullest expression, where the heart and the body unite to celebrate the depth and breadth of love. By differentiating and honoring these two dimensions of intimacy, individuals and couples alike can foster relationships that are rich, balanced, and profoundly nourishing.

The Role of Attachment Styles:
How Attachment Theory Influences Our Sexual Behaviors and Needs, From Secure Bonds to Anxieties in Intimacy

Attachment theory, first developed by John Bowlby and later expanded by Mary Ainsworth, offers profound insights into the way humans form relationships and navigate intimacy. Central to this theory is the understanding that early bonds with caregivers shape not only our emotional framework but also the ways we engage in sexual and romantic relationships. The interplay between attachment styles and sexuality is both complex and deeply rooted in our psychological development, influencing how we express desires, communicate needs, and respond to vulnerability.

Individuals with a secure attachment style, often marked by confidence in their relationships and an ability to balance independence with closeness, typically experience fewer barriers in expressing their sexual needs. They tend to approach intimacy as an extension of emotional trust, which allows them to engage in open and explorative sexual connections. This sense of safety within relationships fosters mutual respect, making it easier to navigate boundaries and preferences. For securely attached individuals, sex often becomes a means of strengthening emotional bonds rather than an avenue for resolving fears or insecurities. The absence of persistent anxiety about rejection or abandonment enables a more fluid and fulfilling exchange, where both partners can feel validated and seen.

Conversely, those with an anxious-preoccupied attachment style often bring heightened emotional intensity into their sexual relationships. Anxiously attached individuals may view sexual intimacy as a critical way to secure reassurance and affirm their partner's commitment.

This can lead to passionate and deeply emotional encounters, it can also create vulnerabilities. The underlying fear of abandonment might manifest in behaviors such as seeking excessive closeness, overinterpreting their partner's actions, or using sex as a tool to anchor the relationship. These tendencies can place a strain on partnerships, as the anxious individual's needs for validation and reassurance may feel overwhelming to a less emotionally intense partner. Consequently, the sexual dynamic may become entangled with the individual's unresolved fears, turning moments of intimacy into a battleground for unspoken insecurities.

The avoidant-dismissive attachment style brings its own unique challenges to the realm of sexual behavior and needs. Avoidantly attached individuals often value independence and emotional self-sufficiency, sometimes to the detriment of close connections. This can manifest in their sexual relationships as a detachment from emotional intimacy, where sex might be pursued for physical pleasure while emotional vulnerability is consciously or subconsciously avoided. These individuals may struggle with opening up fully to their partners, creating a divide where physical closeness does not translate into emotional closeness. Avoidant partners may also shy away from conversations about feelings and needs, leading to misunderstandings or unmet expectations. Despite their apparent indifference, the underlying motivation often stems from a fear of being overwhelmed or losing autonomy, rather than a lack of desire for connection.

For those with a disorganized attachment style, the intersection of attachment needs and sexual behaviors becomes even more intricate. This style, often rooted in early experiences of trauma or inconsistent caregiving, can lead to conflicting desires for both closeness and distance. Individuals with a disorganized style may oscillate between seeking intimacy and pushing it away, creating erratic patterns in their sexual relationships. They might engage in risky or impulsive sexual behavior as a way to cope with unresolved emotional pain or to fulfill a longing for connection that feels safer in short, controlled doses. However, the underlying fear of rejection or betrayal often undermines these efforts, perpetuating cycles of anxiety and detachment that can be difficult to break.

The profound impact, of attachment styles, on sexual behaviors and needs underscores the importance of self-awareness and emotional work in relationships. Recognizing how early attachment experiences shape our approach to intimacy allows for greater understanding of both ourselves and our partners. Through therapy, communication, or personal reflection, individuals can begin to address the patterns and fears rooted in their attachment style. By doing so, it becomes possible to build healthier, more fulfilling sexual relationships where both emotional and physical needs are met.

Ultimately, the intersection of attachment theory and sexuality serves as a powerful reminder of the depth and interconnectedness of human relationships. Our desires, fears, and behaviors are not isolated; they are shaped by the intricate tapestry of our past experiences and emotional landscapes. By exploring and addressing the dynamics of attachment, we can cultivate deeper connections that honor both our vulnerabilities and our capacity for intimacy.

 *Chapter 2 | Sex and Self-Perception*

Body Image and Sexual Confidence:
Exploring the Impact of Body Positivity, Self-Esteem, and
Personal Insecurities on Sexual Satisfaction

The intricate relationship between body image, sexual confidence, and overall self-perception profoundly shapes the contours of an individual's sexual experiences and relationships. At the heart of this dynamic lies the concept of body positivity, a movement advocating for self-acceptance and a more inclusive understanding of beauty. When individuals embrace their physical selves without judgment or shame, their sense of self-esteem often flourishes, paving the way for deeper connections and more fulfilling sexual experiences. However, this journey toward self-acceptance is not always linear. Societal pressures, cultural narratives, and internalized insecurities frequently challenge one's ability to view the body as a vessel of intimacy and pleasure, rather than an object of criticism.

Sexual confidence stems largely from how one perceives their own body. Positive body image is not merely about physical appearance but also about the psychological relationship one maintains with their physical self. When individuals feel confident in their bodies, they are more likely to engage in open and vulnerable sexual expressions. This confidence facilitates communication with partners, allowing individuals to articulate their desires, boundaries, and needs. Conversely, those plagued by negative body perceptions may struggle to fully engage in intimacy, as self-critical thoughts can become barriers to emotional and physical closeness. The lens through which one views their body can either magnify insecurities or illuminate strengths, influencing their approach to sexuality and relationships.

Self-esteem plays a pivotal role in shaping how individuals navigate their sexual identities. A person with high self-esteem often possesses the resilience needed to counteract societal messages that idealize unattainable standards of beauty. This resilience creates space for authentic sexual expression, unencumbered by fears of judgment or rejection. However, individuals with low self-esteem may internalize these societal ideals, leading to feelings of inadequacy that ripple into their sexual lives. Insecurity about one's appearance or sexual capabilities can result in avoidance behaviors, reduced intimacy, or a lack of trust within a partnership. Over time, these patterns can erode the foundation of a healthy sexual relationship, emphasizing the importance of fostering a positive sense of self as a cornerstone for mutual satisfaction.

The influence of body positivity extends beyond the individual, shaping the dynamics of sexual partnerships. When both partners prioritize acceptance and celebration of each other's bodies, the resulting environment of trust and safety encourages deeper emotional and physical bonds. Although, achieving this mutual understanding often requires intentional effort to dismantle harmful narratives and replace them with affirming ones. This process includes recognizing the impact of media representation, challenging stereotypical notions of desirability, and cultivating spaces for honest conversations about vulnerabilities. In doing so, couples can transform potential sources of insecurity into opportunities for connection, strengthening their relationship both inside and outside the bedroom.

Despite the potential benefits of body positivity and high self-esteem, challenges persist in addressing deeply rooted insecurities. Personal histories, including past traumas, societal stigmas, or negative experiences, can leave lasting imprints on an individual's self-image and sexual confidence. Overcoming these obstacles often requires not only personal growth but also support from partners, therapists, or broader communities. Therapy, in particular, can be instrumental in helping individuals reframe negative self-beliefs and develop healthier perspectives. By addressing the intersection of body image, self-esteem, and sexuality, individuals and couples can work toward more satisfying and holistic approaches to intimacy.

Ultimately, the interplay between body positivity, self-perception, and sexual confidence underscores the importance of viewing sexuality as an integrative aspect of human experience. Healthy sexual relationships thrive when individuals feel secure in their own bodies and when partners actively nurture an environment of mutual respect and affirmation. The journey toward this ideal is as complex as it is rewarding, requiring a commitment to self-awareness, vulnerability, and growth. When individuals embrace their physical and emotional selves with compassion and confidence, they unlock the potential for deeper intimacy and enduring satisfaction, setting the stage for a more inclusive and enriching understanding of love and connection.

Sexual Identity and Self-Expression:
Navigating Personal Identity, Orientation, and How Societal Pressures Shape Sexual Behaviors and Desires

Sexual identity is one of the most intimate and multifaceted aspects of human existence. It encompasses how individuals perceive and label their sexual orientation, preferences, and desires. This identity is not static; it evolves with life experiences, introspection, and the influence of broader societal narratives. Sexual orientation, whether it aligns with heterosexuality, homosexuality, bisexuality, pansexuality, or other spectrums, it becomes a cornerstone of how individuals navigate relationships and express their authentic selves. Yet, the path to understanding and embracing one's sexual identity is often fraught with challenges, particularly when societal expectations and pressures are deeply entrenched.

Societal norms and cultural paradigms significantly shape perceptions of sexual identity and self-expression. In many societies, heterosexuality is not just viewed as the default but often as the "ideal" standard of sexual orientation. This pervasive heteronormativity influences how individuals experience their sexuality, sometimes suppressing authentic desires and behaviors in favor of societal acceptance. An example of this would be, individuals who identify as LGBTQ+ may encounter internalized stigma, fear of rejection, or even violence due to their orientation. These pressures often lead to a fracturing of self-identity, forcing people to perform a version of themselves that aligns with societal expectations, rather than living authentically.

At the same time, cultural attitudes toward gender roles often exacerbate these pressures, creating a narrow framework for how sexual behaviors and desires are expressed. With societies where rigid ideas of masculinity and femininity prevail, men and women may feel compelled to conform to predefined roles in their sexual relationships. This can manifest in hyper-masculine behaviors or the sexual objectification of women, perpetuating dynamics that prioritize power over mutual intimacy. For individuals who do not fit into binary gender categories, these pressures become even more pronounced, as their experiences often challenge the foundational assumptions of these norms.

The interplay between sexual identity and self-expression is further complicated by the commercialization and commodification of sexuality. Media portrayals of sexual desire, often filtered through a lens of consumerism, impose unrealistic standards on individuals. From idealized body types to stylized narratives of romance, these portrayals create expectations that are often unattainable, fostering insecurity and dissatisfaction in personal relationships. This disconnect between individual desires and societal ideals can inhibit genuine connection, making it difficult to establish relationships rooted in trust, vulnerability, and mutual respect.

Importantly, societal pressures surrounding sexual identity and expression have tangible impacts on the health of intimate relationships. When individuals suppress their true identities to fit societal molds, they risk developing relationships built on incomplete or inauthentic foundations. Partners may struggle to communicate their needs or desires openly, leading to misunderstandings and a lack of fulfillment. For some, this suppression manifests as a lack of intimacy or emotional distance, further straining the connection between partners. Over time, these patterns can erode the quality of the relationship, as neither partner feels truly seen or understood.

Nevertheless, the journey toward a healthy integration of sexual identity and self-expression is possible and deeply enriching. Recognizing the influence of societal pressures is a critical step in this process, as it allows individuals to challenge the norms that restrict their authentic selves. This requires cultivating environments, both personal and societal, where diversity in sexual identity and orientation is celebrated rather than suppressed. By creating spaces where individuals feel safe to explore and express their sexuality, we enable deeper connections and healthier relationships.

Ultimately, embracing sexual identity and self-expression is not only about personal fulfillment but also about fostering mutual respect and understanding in relationships. It requires confronting the ways in which societal pressures shape desires and behaviors and actively working to dismantle these constraints. Individuals can also forge partnerships that are not just physically satisfying but emotionally and spiritually enriching, rooted in a shared commitment to authenticity and growth. In this way, sexual identity becomes more than a label, it becomes a foundation for connection, liberation, and love.

The Role of Mental Health:
Examining the Influence of Anxiety, Depression, and Stress on Sexual
Functioning and Relationships

Mental health plays a profound role in shaping the contours of human relationships, particularly when it comes to sexual functioning. Sexual health, while often discussed in terms of physiology, is deeply intertwined with psychological well-being. The interplay between mental health issues such as anxiety, depression, and stress, and their impact on sexual relationships, reveals the delicate balance required to maintain healthy intimacy. These mental health challenges not only influence individual sexual functioning but also ripple through the fabric of relationships, affecting communication, trust, and emotional connection.

Anxiety can be a formidable barrier to sexual intimacy, manifesting in ways that disrupt both physical performance and emotional closeness. Individuals experiencing anxiety often grapple with intrusive thoughts, which can amplify insecurities about their bodies or sexual abilities. This mental preoccupation creates a feedback loop: the more one focuses on potential failure, the more likely they are to encounter difficulties such as erectile dysfunction, loss of libido, or an inability to achieve orgasm. Beyond these physical manifestations, anxiety fosters an emotional distance in relationships. Partners may misinterpret avoidance behaviors as disinterest or rejection, leading to misunderstandings and a breakdown in communication. Over time, unresolved anxiety within a relationship can erode the foundation of trust and mutual respect, creating a chasm that is challenging to bridge.

Depression, on the other hand, casts a pervasive shadow over sexual health and relationships. Unlike anxiety, which often heightens arousal but impedes action, depression diminishes the overall desire for intimacy. The characteristic symptoms of depression, low energy, feelings of worthlessness, and anhedonia, strip away the emotional and physical vitality necessary for sexual engagement. Partners of individuals with depression frequently struggle to navigate the silence and withdrawal that accompany this condition. Intimacy, which thrives on vulnerability and connection, is stifled as depressive episodes render emotional sharing nearly impossible. This can lead to a vicious cycle wherein the affected individual feels further isolated due to perceived or actual changes in their partner's behavior, exacerbating depressive symptoms and deepening relational strain.

Stress, a ubiquitous factor in modern life, also significantly impinges on sexual functioning and relationships. While acute stress might momentarily heighten sexual arousal as part of the body's fight-or-flight response, chronic stress has the opposite effect. The prolonged activation of stress hormones such as cortisol disrupts the hormonal balance necessary for healthy sexual functioning. Libido wanes, and the ability to experience pleasure diminishes, creating a frustrating and confusing experience for both partners. Furthermore, stress often diverts energy and attention away from relationships. When one or both partners are consumed by work pressures, financial concerns, or family responsibilities, intimacy is relegated to the background, replaced by irritability or emotional fatigue. Over time, the cumulative effects of stress erode the relational bonds that sustain sexual health, leaving both partners feeling disconnected.

The intersection of anxiety, depression, and stress with sexual health extends beyond their individual effects, as these conditions frequently co-occur, such as the stress of maintaining a demanding career might trigger anxiety, which then leads to depressive symptoms. This cascade of mental health challenges creates a multifaceted impact on sexual functioning and relationships. For some couples, these struggles require mutual patience and understanding, as well as a willingness to address the underlying psychological issues. Mental health interventions, such as therapy or counseling, can play a crucial role in breaking these cycles, fostering healthy relationships, and rekindling intimacy.

Ultimately, healthy sexual relationships depend on an intricate balance between physical and psychological well-being. Mental health challenges such as anxiety, depression, and stress disrupt this balance, highlighting the need for comprehensive approaches to intimacy that encompass both emotional and physiological dimensions. By acknowledging the profound influence of mental health on sexual functioning and relationships, individuals and couples can take meaningful steps toward healing and connection. Through open communication, professional support, and mutual compassion, it is possible to mitigate the impact of these challenges, restoring the intimacy and trust essential to healthy relationships.

Chapter 3 | The Psychology of Desire

Differentiating Love, Lust, and Infatuation: Psychological Distinctions Between Emotional Connection, Physical Desire, and Fleeting Obsession

The human experience of romantic relationships is rich and complex, woven together by threads of love, lust, and infatuation. While these elements can coexist, they are distinct in their origins, manifestations, and outcomes. Understanding the nuances between them provides clarity in navigating relationships and deepens self-awareness. Love, lust, and infatuation operate on different levels of emotional and psychological engagement, each offering unique insights into the human psyche.

Love, at its core, is an enduring emotional connection rooted in mutual respect, trust, and understanding. It transcends superficial attributes, delving into the essence of a person. Love grows steadily, requiring time, shared experiences, and vulnerability. Unlike fleeting emotions, it is characterized by a deep commitment to another's well-being. Psychologically, love engages the brain's reward and attachment systems, fostering feelings of safety and belonging. Neurochemical activity, such as the release of oxytocin and vasopressin, underscores this attachment, reinforcing bonds over time. While love may include physical attraction and passion, these are not its defining features. Love thrives on the values and qualities that inspire admiration and support a sense of shared purpose. Its strength lies in its resilience and capacity to endure challenges, offering stability and emotional fulfillment.

In contrast, lust is a primal force driven by physical desire and sexual attraction. Its foundation lies in biology, fueled by hormones like testosterone and dopamine. Lust often manifests as an intense longing for physical intimacy, and while it can be exhilarating, it is typically short-lived. Unlike love, which evolves over time, lust is immediate and visceral. It is the spark that ignites physical connections but often lacks the depth required for lasting bonds. While lust can coexist with love in a healthy relationship, it is distinct in its singular focus on physical gratification. Lust engages the brain's reward system, generating feelings of excitement and pleasure. However, its transient nature can lead to disillusionment if mistaken for deeper emotional attachment. Lust serves as a reminder of our evolutionary instincts, yet its role in relationships should be balanced by emotional and intellectual compatibility.

Infatuation, meanwhile, resides in the realm of fleeting obsession and idealization. It is characterized by an intense preoccupation with another person, often based on limited knowledge or interaction. Infatuation thrives on fantasy, where the object of affection is elevated to an unrealistic pedestal. Unlike love, which is grounded in reality, infatuation is fueled by imagination and projection. It can evoke powerful emotions, including euphoria and despair, as it hinges on the uncertainty and anticipation of reciprocation. Infatuation often engages the brain's dopamine pathways, creating a cycle of longing and reward. While it can mimic the intensity of love, it lacks the foundation of genuine understanding and commitment. Infatuation tends to fade once the idealized image is challenged by reality, leaving behind clarity or, at times, disillusionment.

Psychologically, these three experiences activate distinct areas of the brain, revealing their unique underpinnings. Love engages regions associated with long-term attachment and emotional bonding, such as the ventromedial prefrontal cortex. Lust activates areas linked to pleasure and reward, like the hypothalamus. Infatuation, with its obsessive qualities, involves heightened activity in regions related to reward anticipation and emotional arousal, such as the ventral tegmental area. These neurobiological differences underscore the importance of distinguishing between these states, as they influence decision-making and relationship dynamics.

While love, lust, and infatuation can coexist in varying degrees within relationships, understanding their distinctions helps individuals navigate their emotions with greater clarity. Love represents the steady anchor, providing security and mutual growth. Lust offers physical excitement and passion, enriching the sensory aspects of connection. Infatuation, though transient, can inspire self-reflection and exploration of desires. Together, they illustrate the multifaceted nature of human relationships, highlighting the interplay between biological impulses, emotional depth, and psychological growth.

Each experience, while unique, contributes to the broader understanding of human connection. Recognizing the differences between love, lust, and infatuation empowers individuals to cultivate healthy relationships. It encourages discernment, fostering choices that align with one's values and long-term goals. Love, in its enduring nature, invites vulnerability and trust, creating a foundation for meaningful partnership. Lust, with its intensity, serves as a reminder of our physicality and the importance of maintaining desire within committed relationships.

Infatuation, despite its fleeting nature, offers lessons in self-awareness, challenging individuals to distinguish between projection and reality.

In the grand tapestry of human emotion, love, lust, and infatuation each play a vital role. They shape our experiences, guiding us through the intricate dance of connection and self-discovery. By exploring their psychological distinctions, individuals gain insight into the forces that drive relationships, paving the way for deeper understanding and fulfillment. Whether seeking a lasting partnership or navigating the early stages of attraction, recognizing these differences serves as a compass, directing us toward authentic and meaningful connections.

Factors That Enhance or Diminish Desire:
Examining External and Internal Factors Such as Stress, Communication,
Novelty, and Emotional Intimacy

Desire, an intricate interplay of physical, emotional, and psychological components, is shaped by a multitude of factors both external and internal. It exists on a spectrum, influenced by circumstances, individual experiences, and relational dynamics. To truly understand desire, one must delve deeply into the ways it can be nurtured or hindered, exploring elements like stress, communication, novelty, and emotional intimacy. These factors do not function in isolation but interact in complex ways that can either fuel or stifle the flames of desire.

- Stress and Its Role in Dampening Desire

Stress is a ubiquitous element of modern life and one of the most significant inhibitors of desire. When the mind is preoccupied with looming deadlines, financial concerns, or interpersonal conflicts, the body's natural response is to shift priorities. The fight-or-flight mechanism, activated by stress, redirects energy away from systems deemed non-essential for survival, such as reproductive and sexual desire. The physiological toll of chronic stress can manifest in hormonal imbalances, fatigue, and a reduced capacity for pleasure.

On an emotional level, stress creates mental barriers that prevent individuals from being fully present in intimate moments. A person overwhelmed by stress may find it difficult to relax, let alone experience the vulnerability needed for genuine connection. Even in the context of a loving relationship, stress can lead to irritability and withdrawal, fostering a sense of distance rather than closeness. This distance can become a self-perpetuating cycle, as diminished emotional intimacy often leads to reduced physical desire, which in turn exacerbates relational stress.

Conversely, managing stress effectively can significantly enhance desire. Practices like mindfulness, meditation, and regular physical activity can mitigate the impact of stress, creating mental and emotional space for intimacy. Partners who actively support one another through stressful times often find that their shared resilience fosters a deeper connection, reinforcing both emotional intimacy and physical attraction.

- The Importance of Communication in Fostering Desire

Communication is the cornerstone of any relationship and a critical factor in the expression and maintenance of desire. Open, honest dialogue about needs, expectations, and boundaries can create a safe space for vulnerability, which is essential for fostering intimacy. When individuals feel heard and understood, they are more likely to experience emotional security—a key ingredient for sustaining desire.

Poor communication, on the other hand, can erode intimacy and breed resentment. Misunderstandings or unspoken expectations often lead to feelings of rejection or inadequacy, which can dampen desire over time. For example, a lack of communication about mismatched sexual needs or preferences may cause frustration or guilt, making it harder for partners to connect physically and emotionally. The absence of dialogue around these sensitive topics can transform a relationship into an emotionally barren landscape where desire struggles to thrive.

Couples who prioritize communication, however, often discover new depths of connection. Regularly checking in with one another, expressing appreciation, and discussing desires openly can reignite passion and foster a sense of partnership. Nonverbal communication, too, plays a significant role in sustaining desire. Gestures of affection, prolonged eye contact, and even the tone of voice can communicate care and attraction, reinforcing the bond between partners.

- Novelty as a Catalyst for Desire

The human brain is wired to respond to novelty, and this extends to matters of desire. In the early stages of a relationship, the thrill of discovery and the excitement of new experiences often fuel intense passion. Over time, however, familiarity can dull this sense of novelty, leading to a decline in desire. This phenomenon, known as the "Coolidge effect," illustrates how the brain's reward system craves variety and stimulation.

Yet, the loss of novelty does not mean desire is doomed to fade. Intentional efforts to introduce new experiences can reignite the spark. Trying new activities together, exploring unfamiliar environments, or even engaging in playful experiments in intimacy can stimulate the brain's reward pathways, rekindling desire. The key lies in maintaining a sense of curiosity and adventure, both about oneself and one's partner.

Without novelty, relationships can fall into predictable routines that feel stagnant over time. This monotony can breed complacency, making it difficult to experience the excitement that often accompanies desire. However, couples who prioritize growth and exploration, both individually and together, can often overcome this challenge. A shared commitment to keeping the relationship dynamic helps maintain a sense of vitality and attraction.

- Emotional Intimacy as the Bedrock of Desire

While novelty provides a spark, emotional intimacy serves as the foundation of enduring desire. Emotional intimacy is the ability to share one's inner world with another and feel a reciprocal sense of closeness and acceptance. This deep connection fosters trust and vulnerability, creating fertile ground for desire to flourish.

When emotional intimacy is lacking, desire often wanes. Feelings of detachment or neglect can lead to a sense of disconnection, making physical closeness feel inauthentic or forced. Over time, unresolved emotional issues can create barriers to desire that are difficult to overcome. For instance, unresolved conflicts or lingering resentments may manifest as disinterest or avoidance in the bedroom.

On the other hand, nurturing emotional intimacy can significantly enhance desire. Acts of empathy, active listening, and mutual support create a sense of partnership that strengthens the emotional bond. This bond, in turn, fuels physical attraction and deepens the overall connection. The more secure and valued individuals feel within a relationship, the more likely they are to experience genuine desire.

Ultimately, desire is not a static phenomenon but a dynamic interplay of multiple factors. Stress, communication, novelty, and emotional intimacy each play a pivotal role in shaping the experience of desire. Understanding and addressing these elements can transform relationships, fostering deeper connections and more fulfilling intimacy. When partners actively engage with these aspects, they not only enhance desire but also build a resilient foundation for long-lasting love and connection.

The Science of Sexual Compatibility:
Analyzing How Personality Traits, Preferences, and Emotional Alignment Affect Long-Term Sexual Harmony

Sexual compatibility is often regarded as one of the cornerstones of a thriving intimate relationship, yet its intricacies extend far beyond surface-level attraction. At its heart lies the dynamic interplay of personality traits, individual preferences, and emotional alignment. These factors converge to shape the quality of physical and emotional intimacy between partners, influencing not only the intensity of their connection but also the longevity of their relationship. Understanding the science of sexual compatibility requires a nuanced exploration of human behavior, psychological needs, and the evolving nature of partnerships over time.

Personality traits serve as the bedrock for sexual compatibility, shaping how individuals approach intimacy and communication within a relationship. Traits such as openness to experience, agreeableness, and emotional stability are particularly influential. Openness, for instance, fosters a willingness to explore new experiences and adapt to a partner's desires, which can enhance the depth of intimacy. Individuals high in agreeableness are more likely to prioritize their partner's satisfaction and emotional well-being, contributing to a harmonious dynamic. Conversely, those with low emotional stability may struggle with anxiety or mood fluctuations, which can create tension and misunderstandings in the sexual realm. The compatibility of two personalities is not just about similarity but also how well differences complement and balance each other, enabling partners to meet each other's needs effectively.

Preferences play a significant role in determining sexual harmony, encompassing a broad spectrum of factors such as physical desires, frequency of intimacy, and attitudes toward experimentation. These preferences are often deeply rooted in an individual's upbringing, cultural influences, and past experiences, making them highly personal. When partners share similar preferences, the likelihood of fulfilling each other's expectations increases, creating a sense of satisfaction and alignment. However, when preferences diverge, open communication becomes vital. Partners must navigate these differences with empathy and compromise, ensuring that neither feels pressured or neglected. Understanding one's own preferences and being attuned to a partner's needs require a level of self-awareness and emotional intelligence, which are critical for sustaining compatibility over time.

Emotional alignment serves as the invisible thread weaving together the physical and psychological dimensions of sexual compatibility. Emotional connection fosters trust, vulnerability, and a sense of security, which are essential for deepening intimacy. This connection often emerges from shared values, mutual respect, and a genuine interest in each other's inner worlds. Without emotional alignment, even the most passionate physical attraction may falter, as the absence of trust and understanding can lead to feelings of isolation or resentment. Emotional alignment also provides a foundation for resolving conflicts and adapting to changes, such as shifts in desire or external stressors, which inevitably arise in long-term relationships.

The science of sexual compatibility also highlights the importance of communication as a dynamic force that bridges gaps and strengthens bonds. Effective communication allows partners to express their needs, set boundaries, and explore shared interests without fear of judgment. It is not uncommon for individuals to struggle with articulating their desires or concerns due to societal taboos or personal insecurities. However, cultivating an open dialogue is essential for addressing mismatches in preferences or resolving conflicts that may hinder compatibility. Over time, this ongoing exchange can deepen mutual understanding and create a safe space for both partners to grow together.

Another critical aspect of sexual compatibility is the role of life stages and external influences. Relationships are not static; they evolve as individuals grow and face new challenges. Factors such as career stress, parenting responsibilities, or health issues can impact sexual dynamics. During these transitions, partners must adapt to each other's changing needs and priorities, which requires flexibility and resilience. Sexual compatibility, therefore, is not merely a fixed trait but a dynamic process that demands continuous effort and adjustment. The ability to navigate these changes together often distinguishes relationships that thrive from those that falter.

Cultural and societal influences further shape perceptions of sexual compatibility, adding another layer of complexity. Cultural norms and expectations can dictate what is considered acceptable or desirable in a relationship, influencing how individuals approach intimacy. For example, societies that prioritize monogamy and long-term commitment may place greater emphasis on emotional alignment and shared values, while others might focus more on physical attraction or sexual experimentation. Understanding these cultural contexts is essential for recognizing how they intersect with personal values and impact relationship dynamics.

Biological and hormonal factors also contribute to sexual compatibility, influencing libido, arousal patterns, and overall sexual satisfaction. Hormonal fluctuations, such as those associated with menstrual cycles, pregnancy, or aging, can affect desire and responsiveness. These physiological changes underscore the importance of patience and adaptability within a relationship. Partners who approach these shifts with understanding and support are better equipped to maintain intimacy and connection, even when faced with challenges.

Finally, the science of sexual compatibility underscores the importance of individual self-awareness and personal growth. Before one can build a compatible partnership, it is essential to understand one's own needs, boundaries, and desires. This self-awareness not only enhances the ability to choose a compatible partner but also fosters healthier communication and deeper emotional connection. Moreover, investing in personal growth allows individuals to bring their best selves to the relationship, contributing to a more fulfilling and harmonious partnership.

In conclusion, sexual compatibility is a multifaceted and dynamic aspect of intimate relationships, shaped by a complex interplay of personality traits, preferences, and emotional alignment. It is not a static quality but an evolving process that requires effort, communication, and mutual respect. By understanding the science behind compatibility, individuals and couples can cultivate deeper connections and navigate the challenges of long-term relationships with greater resilience and fulfillment. Through this journey of exploration and adaptation, sexual compatibility emerges not merely as an outcome but as an ongoing practice that enriches both the physical and emotional dimensions of partnership.

Chapter 4 | Challenges and Growth in Sexual Relationships

Overcoming Sexual Communication Barriers: Techniques for Discussing Needs, Boundaries, and Desires Openly and Without Judgment

Sexual communication is one of the most intimate and challenging forms of dialogue, often shaped by deeply ingrained beliefs, personal experiences, and societal norms. For many, discussing needs, boundaries, and desires openly can feel daunting, leading to misunderstandings, frustration, or even a lack of fulfillment in their relationships. However, cultivating the ability to communicate about such matters is not only empowering but also essential for fostering intimacy and trust. Overcoming barriers to sexual communication begins with understanding the roots of these challenges and developing strategies that promote openness and respect.

At the heart of sexual communication barriers lies a web of fears and assumptions. People often struggle with the vulnerability required to articulate their innermost desires or limits, fearing rejection, judgment, or even ridicule. This fear may stem from past experiences where honesty was met with negativity or from cultural messaging that has stigmatized sexual expression. Furthermore, societal taboos surrounding sexuality often reinforce silence, creating an environment where individuals feel uncomfortable or ill-equipped to engage in meaningful conversations about their needs. Overcoming these hurdles begins with an acknowledgment of these fears and an understanding that vulnerability is not a weakness but a bridge to deeper connection.

One crucial aspect of effective sexual communication is fostering an atmosphere of safety and non judgment. Without this foundation, even the most well-intentioned attempts at dialogue can falter. A safe environment is cultivated when both partners approach the conversation with empathy, patience, and an open mind. This means actively listening without interrupting, validating each other's feelings, and resisting the urge to impose one's opinions or experiences onto the other. Mutual respect is essential, as it ensures that both parties feel valued and heard, even when discussing sensitive or challenging topics. Such an environment allows for the honest exchange of thoughts and feelings, laying the groundwork for growth and understanding.

Another barrier to sexual communication is the lack of a shared vocabulary to articulate needs and desires. Many individuals may struggle to find the right words or feel uncertain about how to convey their feelings without offending or confusing their partner. This can lead to vague or indirect expressions, which often result in miscommunication. Building a shared language involves openly discussing terms, preferences, and feelings in a way that is clear and unambiguous. It also means being willing to educate oneself about sexuality, whether through reading, attending workshops, or engaging in guided conversations with professionals. Expanding one's understanding of sexual topics not only enhances personal confidence but also facilitates clearer, more meaningful communication.

Emotional attunement is another critical component of overcoming sexual communication barriers. Attunement involves being deeply present and responsive to your partner's emotional state, ensuring that the conversation remains balanced and attuned to both parties' needs. This includes recognizing nonverbal cues, such as body language and tone, that may indicate discomfort or hesitation. Attunement also requires practice and mindfulness, as well as a commitment to addressing emotions as they arise rather than allowing them to fester. For instance, if a partner expresses discomfort with a topic, it is essential to pause and explore the reasons behind their reaction instead of pushing forward. Such responsiveness builds trust and creates an environment where difficult topics can be approached with care and sensitivity.

One of the most transformative techniques for overcoming sexual communication barriers is practicing self-awareness and self-compassion. Effective communication begins within; understanding your own needs, boundaries, and desires is a prerequisite for articulating them to another person. This requires introspection and a willingness to confront one's own beliefs and biases about sexuality. Self-compassion plays a vital role in this process, as it allows individuals to forgive themselves for past mistakes or insecurities and approach communication with confidence and a sense of self-worth. When individuals embrace their own humanity and imperfections, they are better equipped to communicate authentically and without fear of judgment.

Timing and context also play significant roles in successful sexual communication. Sensitive topics should be approached in a setting that is conducive to open dialogue, free from distractions or pressures. Choosing the right moment to initiate a conversation can greatly impact its outcome. For instance, discussing sexual needs or boundaries during a conflict or immediately following an intimate encounter may lead to defensiveness or misinterpretation. Instead, choosing a neutral, relaxed environment, where both parties feel at ease, can foster more productive discussions. Patience is key, as these conversations may unfold over time rather than in a single sitting.

Forging a path through sexual communication barriers often involves reimagining the conversation as a collaborative effort rather than a debate or interrogation. Viewing the dialogue as a shared journey toward mutual understanding allows both partners to contribute equally and feel empowered in the process. This perspective encourages curiosity and exploration rather than rigid expectations or ultimatums. It is about discovering common ground and celebrating each other's individuality while striving for deeper intimacy. When both partners approach the conversation with a willingness to learn and grow together, the process becomes less intimidating and more enriching.

Ultimately, overcoming barriers to sexual communication is a transformative endeavor that requires dedication, empathy, and a willingness to embrace vulnerability. It is not a one-time effort but an ongoing process that evolves alongside the relationship. By fostering an atmosphere of safety, building a shared vocabulary, practicing emotional attunement, and cultivating self-awareness, individuals and couples can navigate the complexities of sexual communication with grace and authenticity. These conversations, though challenging at times, hold the potential to deepen intimacy, strengthen bonds, and create a foundation for a fulfilling and mutually satisfying relationship.

Healing Sexual Disconnects:
Addressing Issues Like Mismatched Libidos, Sexual boredom, or Past Traumas to Rebuild Intimacy

Healing sexual disconnects requires careful attention, compassion, and an understanding of the underlying dynamics that contribute to these challenges. When couples experience issues such as mismatched libidos, sexual boredom, or the lingering effects of past traumas, their relationship can suffer in profound ways. However, these struggles do not have to define the partnership. Through openness, effort, and guided exploration, intimacy can be rekindled, creating a space for deeper connection and understanding.

Mismatched libidos are a common issue in relationships, yet they are rarely discussed openly, even among the closest of partners. This silence often stems from societal expectations or personal insecurities about sexual desire. In many cases, mismatched libidos can lead to frustration, feelings of rejection, or a sense of inadequacy. One partner may interpret the other's lower drive as disinterest or even a lack of love, while the partner with less frequent desire may feel pressured or overwhelmed. It's crucial to approach this issue not as a defect in one person but as a dynamic that requires mutual understanding and accommodation. Recognizing that sexual desire ebbs and flows over time can provide a starting point for constructive conversations about needs, preferences, and ways to nurture closeness that feel authentic and satisfying to both partners.

Sexual boredom often arises in long-term relationships, as familiarity can sometimes dampen the thrill of intimacy. While the initial spark of novelty naturally fades, this does not mean that passion must disappear. In fact, enduring relationships offer the opportunity for a deeper, more evolved form of intimacy, one built on trust, shared history, and a willingness to explore together. Addressing sexual boredom involves not only creativity but also vulnerability. It means acknowledging that passion requires nurturing, just like any other aspect of the relationship. However, some couples, this may involve experimenting with new forms of intimacy, whether through open dialogue about fantasies, trying new activities together, or simply setting aside dedicated time to reconnect physically and emotionally. Importantly, there is no one-size-fits-all solution; the path to revitalizing intimacy must be tailored to the unique dynamics of each relationship.

The impact of past trauma on sexual connection is another significant challenge that couples may face. Trauma, whether from previous relationships, childhood experiences, or other sources, often leaves deep emotional scars that can manifest in the context of intimacy. Survivors may struggle with feelings of fear, shame, or detachment, making it difficult to fully engage in a sexual relationship. It is essential to approach this issue with compassion and patience. Healing from these forms of trauma is a process that requires time and, often, professional support. For the partner who has not experienced the trauma, it can be difficult to fully comprehend its effects, but empathy and a willingness to listen are crucial. Creating a safe environment where boundaries are respected and communication is prioritized lays the foundation for rebuilding trust and intimacy. Trauma does not have to permanently inhibit sexual connection; with care and understanding, it is possible to move forward and rediscover closeness.

Communication is at the heart of healing sexual disconnects and for some couples, discussing sex is fraught with discomfort or fear of conflict. Yet, open and honest dialogue is essential for addressing these issues. It's not just about talking, it's about listening, validating each other's feelings, and working collaboratively toward solutions. Couples often benefit from framing these conversations in a way that avoids blame and focuses instead on shared goals. For instance, instead of saying, "You never initiate sex," one might express, "I miss feeling close to you in that way, and I'd like to find ways to bring that back into our relationship." Shifting the focus from criticism to connection can make these conversations more productive and less intimidating.

Rebuilding intimacy also requires intentional effort outside the bedroom. Intimacy is not solely a physical experience; it is deeply emotional and psychological. Small gestures, like holding hands, sharing a laugh, or expressing appreciation, contribute to a sense of closeness that can translate into greater sexual connection. This means prioritizing their relationship amid the demands of daily life. Setting aside time to reconnect, whether through date nights, shared hobbies, or quiet moments of reflection, helps to reinforce the bond that forms the foundation of their intimacy.

Healing sexual disconnects is not a linear process, and setbacks are to be expected. What matters is the commitment to facing these challenges together, with mutual respect and a willingness to grow. Every couple's journey is unique, and the solutions that work for one relationship may not be effective for another. Although, the underlying principles remain the same: communication, empathy, and a shared dedication to rebuilding intimacy. These elements create the conditions for transformation, allowing couples to move from disconnection to a renewed sense of closeness and passion.

Ultimately, addressing issues like mismatched libidos, sexual boredom, or past traumas requires a holistic approach. It involves examining not only the physical aspects of the relationship but also the emotional, psychological, and relational dynamics that contribute to intimacy. It is because this is a process of rediscovery, of oneself, of one's partner, and of the relationship as a whole. Through this journey, couples can find not only healing but also a deeper, more enduring connection, proving that intimacy is not a fixed state but a living, evolving aspect of a loving partnership.

Navigating the Impact of Life Stages:
How Aging, Parenthood, and Health Changes Affect Sexual Dynamics and Ways to Adapt Together

Sexuality is a fundamental part of human connection, an ever-evolving expression of intimacy, desire, and shared vulnerability. Yet, as life unfolds, its expression is often influenced by the stages we encounter: the natural process of aging, the transformative journey of parenthood, and the often unpredictable shifts in health. These changes, while inevitable, can shape and redefine the sexual dynamics within relationships. Understanding and adapting to these transformations not only strengthens bonds but also deepens the emotional and physical connections that sustain us.

Aging introduces a myriad of changes to the body, mind, and emotions, all of which can impact intimacy. Physiological shifts, such as hormonal fluctuations, reduced stamina, or changes in libido, may alter how individuals experience desire and pleasure. Menopause and andropause can bring about physical discomforts like vaginal dryness or erectile challenges, which may discourage intimacy. Yet, aging also brings opportunities. With the maturity that comes from years of shared experiences, couples often develop a deeper emotional connection, allowing for new and creative ways of expressing their sexuality. By focusing on open communication and exploring novel approaches to intimacy, couples can navigate these changes together, transforming potential challenges into avenues for growth and rediscovery.

Parenthood marks another profound shift, affecting not only individual identities but also the dynamics within a partnership. The arrival of children often brings joy and fulfillment, yet it also introduces stress, exhaustion, and a reevaluation of priorities. The demands of parenting can leave little time or energy for intimacy, creating potential tensions in a relationship. The physical aftermath of childbirth, such as temporarily altering a woman's sexual desire or comfort, while the psychological weight of caregiving responsibilities can diminish both partners' focus on each other. Yet, parenthood also offers a chance to cultivate a more profound appreciation for each other's roles. By nurturing their bond and maintaining an ongoing dialogue about their evolving needs, couples can find ways to sustain their sexual connection amidst the realities of raising children. Small gestures, moments of closeness, or even brief shared intimacies can serve as powerful reminders of their partnership.

Health changes, whether temporary or chronic, often serve as critical turning points in sexual relationships. Illnesses, surgeries, or injuries can disrupt established patterns of intimacy, challenging both partners to navigate uncharted territories. Chronic conditions such as diabetes, arthritis, or cardiovascular disease may introduce physical limitations or alter how the body responds to touch and stimulation. Mental health conditions like anxiety or depression can further complicate sexual dynamics by impacting emotional availability and desire. However, such challenges often bring an opportunity to reassess and redefine intimacy. Couples who approach health-related changes with compassion and patience often find that their bond becomes stronger. The key lies in fostering mutual understanding, seeking professional guidance when needed, and prioritizing emotional intimacy as a cornerstone of their connection.

Through each of these life stages, adaptability emerges as the foundation of enduring sexual dynamics. Partners who cultivate a mindset of curiosity, rather than fear, when confronted with change often find themselves better equipped to embrace new ways of relating. Whether it involves experimenting with different forms of physical intimacy, seeking support through therapy, or simply maintaining an ongoing dialogue about each other's needs and desires, the journey of adaptation is deeply enriching. Moreover, recognizing that intimacy is not solely confined to the sexual realm allows couples to build multifaceted connections that encompass physical touch, emotional closeness, and shared experiences.

When navigating the impact of life stages on sexual dynamics, it requires a conscious commitment to growth and connection. Aging, parenthood, and health changes may present challenges, but they also offer profound opportunities to explore the depths of intimacy in ways that transcend physicality. Approach these shifts with empathy, creativity, and an unwavering dedication to partnership, couples can not only sustain their sexual relationship but also cultivate a love that thrives through all the seasons of life.

Chapter 5: | Building a Holistic Sexual Connection

The Role of Trust and Vulnerability:
Fostering Emotional Safety as the Foundation for A Fulfilling Sexual Relationship

The depth and quality of a sexual relationship are profoundly shaped by the emotional bonds between partners. At the heart of these bonds lie trust and vulnerability, two interdependent forces that create the foundation for emotional safety. Emotional safety, in turn, is essential for a fulfilling sexual connection, as it allows individuals to freely express themselves without fear of judgment, rejection, or harm. This interplay between trust, vulnerability, and emotional safety weaves a dynamic and reciprocal cycle, making each essential for the other's existence and growth.

Trust is often seen as the bedrock of any meaningful relationship, but its role in sexual intimacy is particularly crucial. Trust creates the conditions for openness, enabling partners to share their desires, fears, and insecurities. Once trust is established, it becomes possible for individuals to explore both physical and emotional aspects of intimacy without hesitation. An example of this would be when a partner who trusts deeply may feel comfortable sharing fantasies or preferences that they would otherwise guard closely. Without trust, this openness is hindered, as fears of being misunderstood or judged can lead to a guarded and surface-level connection. Thus, trust is not just an emotional comfort; it is a permission slip for authenticity within intimacy.

Vulnerability is equally vital but often more misunderstood. While vulnerability can evoke images of weakness or exposure, in the context of a sexual relationship, it represents courage and self-assurance. To be vulnerable is to present oneself fully, with all imperfections and insecurities, to a partner. This willingness to reveal oneself fosters connection, as it invites the other person to do the same. Vulnerability is inherently risky, as it exposes an individual to potential hurt or rejection. However, it is through this risk that the deepest connections are forged. It communicates a willingness to be seen, heard, and known, which strengthens the relational bond.

Emotional safety arises when trust and vulnerability are nurtured in tandem. Partners can feel emotionally safe, when they know that their feelings, boundaries, and experiences will be met with empathy and care. Emotional safety allows for the full expression of one's sexual self, as the fear of being ridiculed, dismissed, or shamed dissipates. This environment is not merely a passive state but an active and ongoing process, requiring consistent communication, validation, and responsiveness. It is important to understand that when a partner shares a fear or hesitation, the way the other responds can either reinforce safety or erode it. A compassionate response signals acceptance, while dismissiveness can create walls that are hard to overcome.

Building emotional safety in a sexual relationship also requires the acknowledgment and repair of breaches. Trust and vulnerability are not static; they ebb and flow as relationships encounter challenges. Misunderstandings, missteps, or moments of insensitivity are inevitable, but how partners address these moments determines the resilience of their emotional bond. Repair involves acknowledging harm, taking responsibility, and committing to change. This process not only rebuilds trust but often deepens it, as it demonstrates a shared commitment to the relationship's integrity.

Cultural and societal factors can also shape the dynamics of trust and vulnerability in sexual relationships. Many individuals are socialized to view vulnerability as a weakness, particularly in intimate contexts. This belief can lead to emotional walls that hinder connection. Similarly, cultural stigmas around discussing sexuality can create barriers to trust, as individuals may fear judgment or ridicule. Overcoming these societal pressures requires conscious effort, open dialogue, and a redefinition of vulnerability as a strength rather than a liability. When partners work together to dismantle these barriers, they pave the way for a more authentic and fulfilling connection.

In addition to fostering emotional safety, trust and vulnerability contribute to a richer, more nuanced understanding of one another. Through trust, partners develop confidence in each other's intentions and integrity.as well as gain access to the deeper layers of each other's emotional and sexual worlds. This mutual understanding enhances not only the physical aspects of intimacy but also the emotional resonance of the connection. Partners who trust and are vulnerable with one another are more likely to experience intimacy as a holistic and transformative experience, rather than as a mere physical act.

Trust and vulnerability are not endpoints but ongoing processes. They require consistent effort, intentionality, care and by prioritizing these elements, partners can create an environment where emotional safety thrives, enabling them to explore the full spectrum of intimacy together. This journey is not always easy, as it demands confronting fears, insecurities, and societal conditioning. However, the rewards—deeper connection, mutual understanding, and profound fulfillment—are immeasurable. Trust and vulnerability are the keys to unlocking a sexual relationship that is not only physically gratifying but emotionally transcendent.

Exploring Sexual Growth Together:
Introducing Ways Couples Can Grow Sexually, Including Exploring Fantasies, Trying New Experiences, and Attending Workshops

Sexual intimacy is one of the most profound ways couples can connect, and yet, it is often an area that many leave unexplored or undernourished. Over time, life's responsibilities and routines can overshadow the vitality and excitement that once defined a couple's physical connection. Although, far from being a static element of a relationship, sexual growth offers an opportunity for deep connection, mutual understanding, and shared pleasure. Exploring this dimension together requires courage, curiosity, and an openness to step outside of familiar boundaries thus allowing partners to discover new layers of their bond.

One of the most transformative ways to foster sexual growth as a couple is by delving into shared fantasies. Fantasies are not just fleeting thoughts or unattainable ideas; they can be rich sources of insight into a person's desires and untapped dimensions of their sexuality. When partners feel safe to express these inner thoughts, a powerful connection can form, rooted in trust and vulnerability. Discussing fantasies, however, requires careful navigation. This process is not about pressuring one another or judging what is shared but about creating a safe and accepting space where even the most unconventional ideas can be heard. Sharing fantasies might begin with casual conversations, perhaps sparked by a movie scene or a story, slowly building confidence in the exchange. The act of listening without judgment and reciprocating with one's own thoughts opens a pathway to not only explore new possibilities but to deepen emotional intimacy.

Trying new experiences is another avenue for sexual growth that can invigorate and enrich a relationship. Over time, routines may establish themselves within a couple's intimate life, and while predictability can provide comfort, it can also lead to stagnation. Introducing new elements, however small, can reignite the spark and create excitement. This might involve experimenting with new environments, positions, or techniques, or exploring tools and accessories that encourage playful interaction. What is most important is not the specifics of the activity but the shared journey of discovery, which is a process that is less about achieving perfection or mastery and more about embracing curiosity and enjoying the unpredictability of exploring together. New experiences can foster laughter, surprise, and a renewed sense of partnership, as each person learns to trust the other with their emerging preferences and boundaries.

For couples looking to dive deeper into their sexual growth, attending workshops or retreats can be a particularly meaningful step. These spaces, designed to foster intimacy and education, provide an environment where couples can engage with expert guidance and structured activities. Workshops may focus on a range of topics, from enhancing communication to learning techniques for deeper physical connection. The benefit of such experiences is twofold: couples gain practical skills and insights while also stepping outside their usual context, allowing them to view their relationship from a fresh perspective. Often, the communal aspect of these settings can also be empowering, as couples realize they are not alone in their challenges or desires. This shared journey of learning and self-discovery can ripple into other aspects of their relationship, cultivating a sense of partnership that transcends the physical realm.

Embarking on a journey of sexual growth together is not without its challenges. Vulnerabilities may emerge, and insecurities can surface as partners navigate unfamiliar territory. However, these moments of discomfort are opportunities for profound connection and growth. By addressing fears and uncertainties openly, couples can transform potential stumbling blocks into stepping stones. Patience and kindness toward oneself and one's partner are essential during this process. Growth, after all, is not a linear path but a winding journey filled with discovery, missteps, and moments of profound connection. Each attempt to understand one another more deeply, whether successful or not, is an act of love and commitment.

The journey toward sexual growth is deeply personal and varies from couple to couple. What works for one pair may not resonate with another, and that's part of the beauty of the process. It's not about following a prescribed path but about finding what feels authentic and meaningful for both partners. For some, growth might mean rekindling lost passion; for others, it could involve exploring aspects of their sexuality they've never acknowledged before. The key is to remain open and adaptable, recognizing that growth is not a destination but an ongoing process of evolution.

Exploring sexual growth as a couple is about more than physical pleasure. It's about building a relationship that thrives on mutual respect, trust, and a willingness to evolve together. Exploring sexual growth is an opportunity to create a shared narrative of intimacy and connection that is uniquely yours. As partners embark on this journey, they may find not only new dimensions of their sexual relationship but also a deeper appreciation for the love and bond they share.

Cultivating Long-Term Intimacy:
Strategies for Maintaining Sexual and Emotional Connections Over Time,
Balancing Routine with Excitement

Intimacy, in its truest form, is the foundation of any meaningful relationship. It transcends mere physical attraction or fleeting emotional highs, delving deep into the realms of vulnerability, trust, and enduring connection. Cultivating long-term intimacy requires a conscious effort to nurture both sexual and emotional bonds, a journey that evolves as two individuals grow and change over time. Intimacy is not a static achievement but a dynamic process, requiring balance, attentiveness, and creativity.

At the heart of long-term intimacy lies the concept of connection, one that exists on multiple levels. Emotional intimacy, which stems from mutual understanding, trust, and shared experiences, provides the groundwork for deeper sexual intimacy. When a couple invests in fostering emotional closeness, they create a space where vulnerabilities are embraced, fears are softened, and love flourishes. This emotional foundation is the invisible thread that ties partners together, making their bond resilient to the inevitable stresses and challenges of life.

Sexual intimacy, on the other hand, is an expression of the emotional connection but also serves as its own vital entity. In a long-term relationship, sexual intimacy can become a mirror reflecting the health of the emotional connection. While early stages of love are often marked by intense passion and novelty, maintaining a fulfilling sexual relationship over time requires adaptability and an ongoing commitment to understanding each other's desires and boundaries. It's not merely about keeping passion alive but about evolving together in ways that honor each partner's individuality and shared needs.

Routine, often seen as the enemy of excitement, can actually be a powerful ally in nurturing intimacy. In the stability of routine lies the opportunity for ritual, those small, intentional acts that remind partners of their commitment and love for one another. A morning coffee prepared just the way your partner likes it, a shared walk at sunset, or a recurring date night may seem mundane on the surface, but these practices create a steady rhythm of connection. These rituals form a backdrop of safety and consistency against which deeper explorations can unfold.

Yet, routine must be balanced with novelty to keep the spark of intimacy alive. Excitement, in this context, isn't necessarily about grand gestures or dramatic changes; it can be found in the small surprises and explorations that punctuate the rhythm of daily life. Trying a new activity together, exploring a fresh perspective on an old conversation, or even venturing into uncharted territories in the bedroom can reignite curiosity and deepen the connection. Novelty, when combined with the safety of routine, creates a dynamic interplay that keeps the relationship vibrant and alive.

Communication is the lifeblood of maintaining both emotional and sexual intimacy. It is not enough to assume that your partner understands your needs or that the relationship will thrive on autopilot. Open, honest dialogue fosters a culture of vulnerability and mutual respect. Conversations about feelings, aspirations, and even fears strengthen the emotional bond, while discussions about desires and boundaries enrich the sexual connection. Importantly, such communication is not limited to words, it extends to body language, gestures, and the silent affirmations found in a loving gaze or a reassuring touch.

Another key aspect of sustaining long-term intimacy is the willingness to embrace change. As individuals, we are constantly evolving, shaped by life's experiences and challenges. In a long-term relationship, partners must allow space for growth, both individually and as a couple. This includes recognizing and addressing shifts in emotional needs or sexual preferences without judgment or resistance. Adaptability becomes an act of love, a recognition that nurturing intimacy means not clinging to who we were but celebrating who we are becoming.

Equally important is the role of self-awareness and self-care in sustaining intimacy. A fulfilling relationship requires two whole individuals who bring their best selves to the partnership. When we neglect our own emotional or physical needs, it becomes harder to connect authentically with a partner. Self-care, whether through personal reflection, physical well-being, or pursuing passions outside the relationship, fuels the energy and presence needed to nurture intimacy. It is a reminder that loving oneself is an integral part of loving another.

Challenges are inevitable in any long-term relationship, but they need not be barriers to intimacy. In fact, navigating difficulties together can deepen the bond between partners. Conflict, when approached with empathy and a willingness to understand, becomes an opportunity for growth. It is through these moments of tension that couples can learn more about themselves and each other, building a resilience that strengthens their connection. Intimacy thrives not in the absence of challenges but in the shared commitment to overcome them together.

At its core, cultivating long-term intimacy is an act of intention, presence and is the deliberate choice to prioritize connection amidst the demands of daily life, to see one's partner as both a constant and a mystery, deserving of love and discovery. It requires a blend of steadiness and spontaneity, of grounding and exploration, creating a partnership that is both a safe haven and a space for growth.

Long-term intimacy is a journey, not a destination. It is an ongoing dance of attunement, where partners move together through the rhythms of life, finding balance between the familiar and the new. With patience, creativity, and a shared commitment, the bond of intimacy can not only endure but deepen, becoming a source of joy, strength, and profound connection for years to come.